Glenn N. Galler

My Recruiting Secrets

for Engineering Students

Copyright © 2013 by Glenn N. Galler. All rights reserved.

This book or any portion thereof may not be reproduced or used in any manner whatsoever without the express written permission of the publisher except for the use of brief quotations in a book review.

Printed in the United States of America

First Printing, 2013

Photography: iStockphoto/ThinkStock

ISBN: 978-1491035986

ISBN: 1491035986

Book Design: Grace W. Galler

Table of Contents

INTRODUCTION 1

THE RECRUITING CYCLE 5
    "Sweet Spots" in the Recruiting Cycle 7
    Looking for a Job Late in the Cycle 8

THE RESUME 11
    Naming Your Resume File 13
    The Length of Your Resume 14
    The "10 Second" Rule 15
    Knowing What is in Your Resume 16
    Include Past, Present, but not Future 17
    Formatting the BS and MS Resumes 18
    Formatting the Ph.D. Resume 22

BS AND MS RESUMES 27
    Name and Address Section 29
    Objective Section 30
    Education Section 32
    Education Special Topics Section 41
    Work Experience, Research Experience, Academic Projects Section .. 48
    Leadership Section 60
    Skills Section 63
    Honors and Awards Section 65

PH.D. RESUMES 67
    Dissertation Section 69
    Patents Section 70
    Fellowships Section 71
    Grants Section 72
    Certifications Section 73
    Publications Section 74
    Conference Abstracts Section 75
    Conference Presentation Section 76

CAREER FAIR ... 77

- Know the Different Types of Recruiters ... 80
- Good Questions to Ask Recruiters ... 82
- Talking about Your Multiple Majors ... 83
- Know the Jobs for your Major ... 85
- Preparation for International Students ... 86
- What Recruiters Ask International Students ... 87
- What International Students Can Ask Recruiters ... 88
- Multiple Recruiters from the Same Company ... 89
- What Do You Do When It Is Your Turn ... 90

INTERVIEWING ... 93

- Research the Company ... 95
- Develop "Tell Me About Yourself" ... 96
- Know how Behavioral Interviews Work ... 101
- Prepare Questions for the Interviewer ... 105
- The Interview Day ... 107
- Know Next Steps After the Interview ... 109

INTERNSHIPS/CO-OPS ... 111

- Knowing Who to Impress ... 113
- Keeping Your Manager Informed ... 114
- Creating Your Status Report ... 116
- Dealing with a Manager Change ... 118
- Continuing Work after an Internship or Co-op ... 119
- Saving Important Contact Information ... 120

FULL-TIME JOBS ... 121

- Keep Your Manager Informed ... 123
- Think About Your Long-Term Goals ... 124
- Understand How Your Appraisal Works ... 125
- Tell Your Manager You Want a Promotion ... 126

CONCLUSION ... 129

This book is dedicated to my father, Bernard A. Galler, Ph.D. Before his death in 2006, he spent fifty one years at the University of Michigan in Math and Computer Science. He served as the Department Chairman, a Ph.D. Advisor, and as the Undergraduate Program Advisor. He worked with students at all levels because he was passionate about their success.

Acknowledgments

I would like to thank Xin Guan for sharing her ideas on writing books, including the suggestion to develop the "My Recruiting Secrets" blog (www.glenngaller.com) prior to writing this book.

I would like to thank Bruce Galler, Elaine Levine, and Enid Galler for their excellent editing of my book.

I would like to thank Grace Galler for providing her creativity, graphical expertise, and dedication to the design of this book.

I would like to thank my wife, Carol, and the rest of my family, who encouraged me to write this book.

Introduction

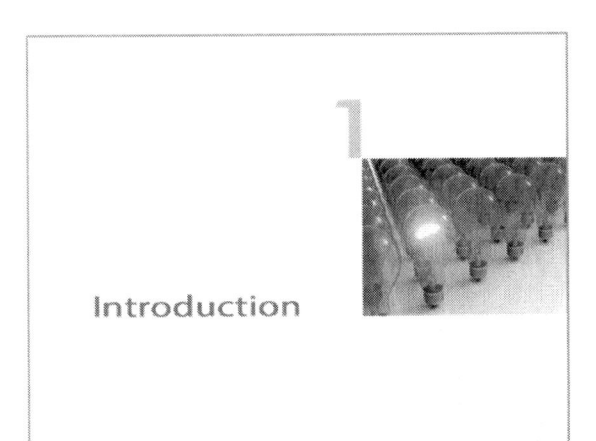

I really wanted to be the Campus Recruiting Manager for the IBM Software Group for the University of Michigan. I grew up in Ann Arbor, Michigan, and my father had been a professor in Computer Science for 43 years. I received my BS degree in Computer Science from the University of Michigan and I am a life-time member of the University of Michigan Alumni Association.

In 1997, I was a new manager of an IBM software development group in San Jose, California. The IBM Campus Recruiting Manager for the University of Michigan had held the position for many years and he was not about to give it up. I contacted him and offered to help him with his recruiting efforts. I told him all of the reasons why it would be great for him to take me to Ann Arbor, Michigan. He was very nice in his responses. He would just say, "Thanks, but I have it covered". I persisted and sent him a note once-a-month with my offer to help with his recruiting, but the response was always the same.

Persistence can lead to good things. In 1998, I returned from the winter break and found a blue binder in front of my door with a yellow note on the front. It read, "I retired; it's yours!". I opened the binder and found a picture of the University of Michigan campus and understood that I was the new Campus Recruiting Manager for the University of Michigan. Since then, I have received many notes from recent University of Michigan graduates offering to help with my recruiting and I am very polite when I say, "Thanks, but I have it covered."

INTRODUCTION

It has been over 15 years since I started recruiting at the University of Michigan. To understand the complexities of recruiting, you have to do the work of a recruiter and also experience working in the field of Engineering. I have done both in my career.

In my 31 years with IBM, I have been a team leader multiple times in software development. I have been a manager in software development in the Bay Area in California where I hired several college graduates. I have been a technical consultant for large and sophisticated customers, and I often speak at major conferences. I have also been a project manager for a product with over 200 people on the development team. From 1992 to 1997, I lived in London, England, and was the Program Manager for a large software product in Europe, the Middle East, and South Africa where I gained international exposure and work experience.

As a recruiter, I have attended over 30 Career Fairs in the past 15 years and given over 390 formal student interviews. I have participated in 12 all-day mentoring sessions for the University of Michigan Alumni Association. I have participated by invitation on university panels for both the University of Michigan Engineering School and the University of Michigan Ross School of Business, focusing on topics ranging from interview preparation and resume creation, to helping student groups interact better with companies. I have given a number of technical talks on Database Technology, which is my area of expertise, and I have given several lectures to students on how to succeed in the recruiting process. While most of my recruiting has been at the University of Michigan, I have also recruited at the University of Wisconsin in Madison and the University of California in Orange County.

This book is a collection of advice and observations gained from three decades of experiences in recruiting and leading projects. I hope this book will help you get started in your career by revealing to you the secrets of the recruiting process.

2

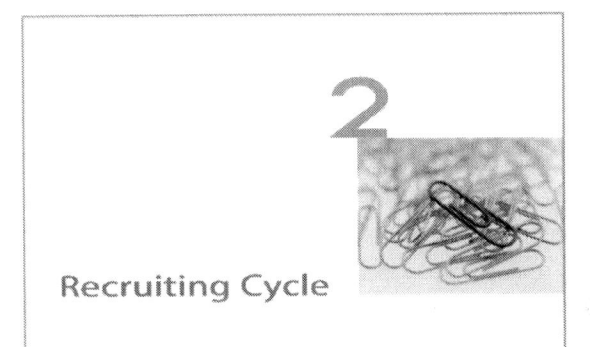

Recruiting Cycle

The recruiting timing cycle is complicated for both companies and students. Many recruiters will plan their on-campus activities in the summer and begin talking to students in September. The process is constantly evolving as students receive and accept offers and as business needs change. Hiring managers understand the flux in the system and try very hard to hire students as early in the process as they can to ensure their hiring opportunities are not withdrawn for business reasons.

As students, it isn't necessary to understand the complexities of a company's recruiting process. Students just need to focus on getting the right job in the right company.

The Timing in the Recruiting Process

1. "Sweet Spots" in the Recruiting Cycle
2. Looking for a Job Late in the Cycle

1 "Sweet Spots" in the Recruiting Cycle

The best times for an engineering student to find a job are in October and November, because that is when there are the most hiring opportunities available. The second best time to land a job is between January and early March. There is very little recruiting going on in December or after April though there may still be jobs available.

I have met many students who think that hiring for full-time positions occurs only in the Fall and hiring for summer internships and co-ops is done only in the Spring or Winter terms. This is true for some companies, but many companies fill both full-time and internship positions any time during the school year starting in September. Your recruiting should begin in the Fall term and should carry on until you find the right position for your needs, regardless of whether you are seeking a full-time job, summer internship, or co-op position.

2 Looking for a Job Late in the Cycle

If April arrives and you still have not lined up a position for the summer, there is still hope; however, the ball switches to your court. You have to contact recruiters yourself. It's a very good idea when you are talking to recruiters in the Fall and Winter terms to ask for their contact information. A recruiter may formally give it to you or you can just look it up online if you know the recruiter's name.

Last summer, I had a student contact me during the summer because his plans had changed; he had followed his fiancée out to California where she planned to get her Ph.D. He had graduated and needed a job in their new city. The student was surprised when I told him that I could include him in the upcoming Fall hiring, and furthermore, I would place him at the head of the list giving him more exposure. He went from having no job to being first in line just because he knew my contact information and took the initiative to contact me.

The business cycle and the recruiting cycle do not always coincide with each other. A new project requiring new staffing can occur at any time during the year. Last April, I was contacted by a manager who was staffing up a new project and she specifically wanted to interview students from my university. Unfortunately, I no longer knew whether the students I had interviewed were still looking for jobs, and I had no good way of contacting them.

When you contact a recruiter on your own initiative, I recommend that you start the conversation with a specific statement about your situation. For example, you can say, "I'm just following up to see if you have any current job openings." You can also say, "My plans have changed. I won't be taking a summer course now and I would like to find a summer job in your company." Finally, you can say, "I decided not to attend graduate school and now I need to find a full-time job."

If you are still looking for a job in April, take the initiative and contact the recruiters you have met during the year. It is possible that they will appreciate hearing from you.

3

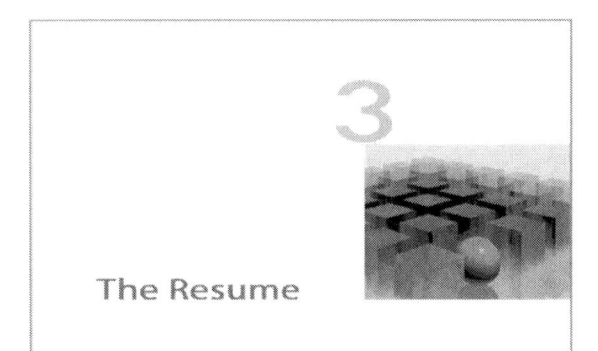

The Resume

The resume is the key to recruiting. You use the resume at the Career Fair, the interview, when networking, and throughout your career. It should be updated each term you are in school.

Your resume is your first opportunity to introduce yourself to a recruiter. It is a good idea to carry it with you at all times while you are on campus because you never know when you are going to meet a recruiter on campus. As recruiters, we no longer scan printed resumes; we expect to receive online resumes from you or the university. However, we do look at hardcopy resumes given to us all of the time.

The Keys to Creating a Resume

1. Naming Your Resume File
2. The Length of Your Resume
3. The "10 Second" Rule
4. Knowing What is in Your Resume
5. Include Past, Present, but not Future
6. The BS and MS Resume
7. The Ph.D. Resume

1 Naming Your Resume File

Your online resume will be passed among hiring managers and Human Resources personnel so it is a good idea to name the file:

"Firstname_Lastname_Resume.PDF"

For example, my resume is named:

"Glenn_Galler_Resume.PDF".

It is very important to use the PDF format because not all companies use Microsoft Word® or the recruiter might not have the latest version of Microsoft Word® which uses ".docx" in place of ".doc" as the file extension.

However, all recruiters and companies have the ability to read PDF files and PDF format files are portable and read the same on all operating systems including Windows®, Macintosh®, Unix® and Linux®.

2 The Length of Your Resume

If you are seeking a BS or MS degree, your resume should fit on one page. When a BS or MS resume contains multiple pages, it is usually because it is not well-organized or it contains too much information. The resume doesn't need to say everything about you. It just needs to convey what is important and relevant for the position you are seeking.

A resume for a Ph.D. candidate will usually have multiple pages because it will include several additional sections.

When you are a Freshmen or a Sophomore, you may need to include information from your high school experience. But as you move through college, it is important to replace the high school information with experiences you have during college. Your high school accomplishments got you into the university, but it is your college accomplishments that will get you your internships and initial full-time position.

3 The "10 Second" Rule

As a recruiter, I try to visualize a chronological outline of students through their resumes, and I need to be able to do this in 10-15 seconds. There are three times when I most often look at a resume. The first is at the Career Fair where students present me with their resume and I tell them about my company and where they might fit. The second time is when I have a stack of resumes and I need to select a few prospects for my interview schedule. I will literally sort through hundreds of resumes. The third time is just before and during the actual interview with the student in the room. In each of these situations, my review of the resume has to be done quickly.

During the interview, a well-organized and consistent resume should be sized up in about 10-15 seconds, leaving the remaining time for a good discussion.

4 Knowing What is in Your Resume

One of the most important rules to follow is to be able to converse enthusiastically and knowledgably about every word you put in your resume. When I ask a student about a project listed on the resume and I hear, "That project was a long time ago and I don't remember it very well", I wonder why the student listed it on their resume. You should be able to speak positively and with some excitement about every entry on your resume. The information on the resume is your opportunity to control the flow of the interview and to show your excitement about your studies.

As you move through school, it is a good idea to update the projects on your resume so that they remain fresh in your mind. For students in the Ph.D. program, it is especially important to review the publications and conference abstracts on your resume prior to interviews so that you remember them.

5 Include Past, Present, but not Future

You can describe your current and past projects and work assignments on your resume. For example, if you are currently enrolled in a class, you can list this class on your resume in the Education section. However, you should not include any information about work you have not yet started. For example, if you are taking a course for which there is a great final project, but you have not yet started it, you should not include this project on your resume. If you really want the recruiter to hear about this project, you can bring it up when the recruiter asks, "What courses are you taking now?" which is a very common question. In response, you can say "I'm taking Aerodynamics ... and I would like to tell you about the final project which I will begin shortly."

If you are an International student and you have filed for Permanent Residency but have not yet received it, you can mention this on your resume and point out the status of your application.

6 Formatting the BS and MS Resumes

There is no single format that is best for an Engineering resume, but some formats do work better than others. I like to see a resume split into specific sections. For BS and MS degree students, an example of a well-formatted resume is shown in Figure 1. If you use this format, you will find it easy to include the right information on your resume.

In this format, each section is capitalized and underlined. I place all of the dates in the right column and no other information in the right column other than the dates. A good resume also includes a fair amount of "white space" for readability. A well-formatted resume is also consistent. For example, if you start out using 3-character dates (ex. Apr, 2014), then it is good to continue using them throughout the resume. Finally, it is very important to proof-read your resume so that it doesn't include any errors like spelling mistakes. Many recruiters see simple resume errors as a "lack of attention to details". You should always ask several other people to proof-read your resume with fresh eyes.

Jane Smith

734-555-1212   185 Arctic Lane
jsmith@umich.edu   Ann Arbor, MI 48105

OBJECTIVE
Seeking an internship in Computer Science Engineering   Available: May-Aug, 2013

EDUCATION
University of Michigan, Ann Arbor, Michigan   Apr, 2014
B.S.E., Computer Science, Minor in Economics
GPA = 3.45/4.00
Dean's List = 2011, 2012
Significant Coursework:
- Database Theory (484)
- Advanced O-O Programming (371)
- Operating Systems (332)
- Compiler Design (411)

WORK EXPERIENCE
Tolstoy Networks, San Jose, California   May – Aug, 2011
Software Intern
- Led a team of 4 engineers to develop a software monitor
- Presented performance results to management team

ACADEMIC PROJECTS
University of Michigan, Ann Arbor, Michigan   Fall, 2012
Database Theory (484): *"Indexing an XML Database"*
- Created relational and XML object mappings
- Developed algorithm to remove sparsely covered cell groupings

LEADERSHIP
University of Michigan, Ann Arbor, Michigan   Fall, 2012
Undergraduate Student Instructor: Intro to Data Structures (280)
- Led a discussion section with 23 students

SKILLS
Computer Languages:	Java, C++, C, Objective-C, .NET (C#), Perl
Environments:	UNIX, Android, Windows, Linux
Spoken Languages:	Mandarin

HONORS AND AWARDS
- China Undergraduate Mathematical contest (1st Place)   Dec, 2012
- EPICS-AMD, Excellence in Team Performance Award   Apr, 2012
- University of Michigan EECS Outstanding Service Award   Jan, 2012

Figure 1: Well-Formatted BS and MS Degree Resume

To create this sample resume, I used the Microsoft Word® Table feature with "no borders". This allows the lines of the resume to be aligned correctly. When you use "no borders", you have to enable "View Gridlines" to see the actual table borders. In Microsoft Word® 2010, you must click on one of the tables under the Table Tools Layout tab and then choose the View Gridlines option as shown in Figure 2.

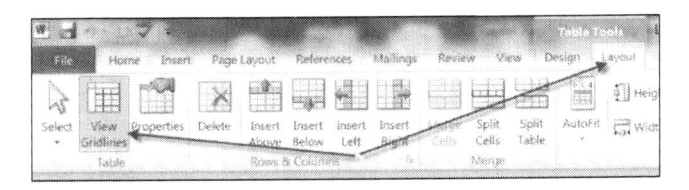

Figure 2: Microsoft Word 2010 "View Gridlines"

An example of a resume with "View Gridlines" enabled is shown in Figure 3.

Jane Smith

| 734-555-1212 | 185 Arctic Lane |
| jsmith@umich.edu | Ann Arbor, MI 48105 |

OBJECTIVE

| Seeking an internship in Computer Science Engineering. | Available: May-Aug, 2013 |

EDUCATION

University of Michigan, Ann Arbor, Michigan	Apr, 2014
B.S.E., Computer Science, Minor in Economics	
GPA = 3.45/4.00	
Dean's List = 2011, 2012	
Significant Coursework:	
• Database Theory (484) • Operating Systems (332)	
• Advanced O-O Programming (371) • Compiler Design (411)	

WORK EXPERIENCE

Tolstoy Networks, San Jose, California	May – Aug, 2011
Software Intern	
• Led a team of 4 engineers to develop a software monitor	
• Presented performance results to management team	

ACADEMIC PROJECTS

University of Michigan, Ann Arbor, Michigan	Fall, 2012
Database Theory (484): *"Indexing an XML Database"*	
• Created relational and XML object mappings	
• Developed algorithm to remove sparsely covered cell groupings	

LEADERSHIP

University of Michigan, Ann Arbor, Michigan	Fall, 2012
Undergraduate Student Instructor: Intro to Data Structures (280)	
• Led a discussion section with 23 students	

SKILLS

Computer Languages:	Java, C++, C, Objective-C, .NET (C#), Perl
Environments:	UNIX, Android, Windows, Linux
Spoken Languages:	Mandarin

HONORS AND AWARDS

• China Undergraduate Mathematical contest (1st Place)	Dec, 2012
• EPICS-AMD, Excellence in Team Performance Award	Apr, 2012
• University of Michigan EECS Outstanding Service Award	Jan, 2012

Figure 3: BS/MS Resume with Microsoft Word Tables

7 Formatting the Ph.D. Resume

The Ph.D. resume is usually longer than one page because it contains more sections and the student is in school longer. While the Ph.D. resume is longer, it is still important for it to be concise and well-organized. It is a good idea to format the resume so that new sections are not split across page boundaries. It is okay to leave some blank space at the bottom of each page to allow this to happen. An example of a well-formatted Ph.D. resume starts with Figure 4 and continues on with Figure 5 and Figure 6.

Jane Smith

734-555-1212
jsmith@umich.edu

155 Artic Lane
Ann Arbor, MI 48105

OBJECTIVE

Seeking an fulltime position in researching XML database systems.   Available: May, 2014

EDUCATION

University of Michigan, Ann Arbor, Michigan   Apr, 2014
Ph.D, Computer Science
Advisor: Samuel Huggins, Simon A. Shuster Professor of Computer Science
Dissertation: *"Identifying Transformations in XML Indices"*

> This dissertation demonstrates that a hierarchical abstraction of an XML database system can be simplified by first mapping the relational meta-data. We define the transformation as a mapping of meta-columns and demonstrate iteration through sequencing over complex structures. We introduce the concept of "XML Index Transformation" and demonstrate that each atomic property persists in subsequent levels of abstraction.

University of Michigan, Ann Arbor, Michigan   Aug, 2010
M.S.E., Computer Science
GPA = 7.9/9.0 (Scale: 9.0=A+, 8.0=A, 7.0=A-)
Advisor: Antoine Lyon, Basel T. Simons Professor of Computer Science
Thesis: *"Analyzing Asynchronous Arrays in XML Indices"*

University of Michigan, Ann Arbor, Michigan   Jun, 2008
B.S.E., Electrical and Computer Science Engineering

WORK EXPERIENCE

Tolstoy Networks, San Jose, California   May – Aug, 2011
Software Intern
- Led a team of 4 engineers to develop a software monitor
- Presented performance results to management team

Computer Softworks, Austin, Texas   May – Aug, 2010
Software Intern
- Designed a performance monitor using Eclipse technology
- Deployed monitor on four development platforms

Figure 4: Well-Formatted Ph.D. Resume (Page 1)

LEADERSHIP

University of Michigan, Ann Arbor, Michigan — Fall, 2012
Graduate Student Instructor (GSI): Advanced Database Theory (584)
- Led discussion section with 23 students

SKILLS

Computer Languages: Java, C++, C, Objective-C, .NET (C#), Perl
Environments: UNIX, Android, Windows, Linux
Spoken Languages: Spanish, French

HONORS AND AWARDS

- EPiCS-AMD, Excellence in Team Performance Award — Dec, 2012
- University of Michigan EECS Outstanding Service Award — Apr, 2011
- Michigan Undergraduate Mathematical contest (1st Place) — Jan, 2008

PATENTS

Software Patent: US 7,552,361 — Jun 23, 2009
Inventors: J. Smith, G. Galler
Title: *"Software Testing Optimization Apparatus and Method"*

FELLOWSHIPS

2012 Ford Foundation Fellowship Program — 2012
University of Michigan, Computer Science

GRANTS

National Science Foundation (NSF), (CCR-977524) — Jan – May, 2011
Funding for the University of Michigan workshop on XML Transformations

National Science Foundation (NSF), (BNT-125524) — Sep, 2010
Funding for the software and systems conference in Berlin, Germany

CERTIFICATIONS

IBM Certified Solution Developer — Jan, 2008
XML 3.4 Database Administrator

IBM Certified System Administrator — Jun, 2008
XML 3.4 System Performance Analyst

Figure 5: Well-Formatted Ph.D. Resume (Page 2)

THE RESUME

PUBLICATIONS

Database Technical Resource (DTR) — Aug, 2012
Authors: J. Smith, B. Smithen, J. Lickey, X. Gan, A. Worthington
Title: *"Examining XML from the Source Level"*
Issue: 27(11), 1079-1101

ACM Multimedia Systems — May, 2012
Authors: J. Smith, B. Strangelove, J. Workey, X. Gan, T. Pavela
Title: *"Isolating the XML Transformation"*
Issue: 10(2), 179-184

Computer Graphics Bulletin (CGB) — Dec, 2011
Authors: J. Smith, B. Randall, S. Wagner, X. Gan, W. Alveystein
Title: *"Relating XML Indices with Relational Indices"*
Issue: 14(16), 83-101

CONFERENCE ABSTRACTS

IEEE International Symposium on Database Systems, Washington, DC — Aug 19 – 25, 2011
Authors: J. Smith, B. Smithen, J. Lickey, X. Gan, A. Worthington
Title: *"Examining XML from the Source Level"*

ISMRM 17th Scientific Meeting and Exhibition, Berlin, Germany — May 2 – 5, 2011
Authors: J. Smith, B. Strangelove, J. Workey, X. Gan, T. Pavela
Title: *"Sequencing the XML Hierarchy"*

CONFERENCE PRESENTATIONS

14th European Software Conference, Graz, Austria — Mar 4 – 8, 2011
Title: *"Demonstrating Decay in XML Sequencing"*

Information Software Symposium, Los Angeles, California — Nov 21 – 25, 2010
Title: *"Sequencing the XML Hierarchy Through Iteration"*

Figure 6: Well-Formatted Ph.D. Resume (Page 3)

To create this sample Ph.D. resume, I used the Microsoft Word® Table feature with "no borders". This allows the lines of the resume to be aligned correctly. When you use "no borders" you have to enable "View Gridlines" to see the actual table borders as shown in Figure 2.

4

BS and MS Resumes

I have seen and reviewed hundreds of resumes over the years and I have determined that a well-organized BS or MS degree resume should contain some or all of the following sections in this order:

1. Name and Address
2. Objective
3. Education
4. Work Experience
5. Research Experience
6. Academic Projects
7. Leadership
8. Skills
9. Honors and Awards

It is not necessary to use all of these sections and it is very important to keep a BS or MS degree resume to one page. When it is done well, your resume can be very impressive to a recruiter.

1 Name and Address Section

Your name and contact information belong at the top of your resume. You should include your home or cell phone numbers or both, your student address, and a valid email address. It is important to check that the font used shows letters like "i" and "I" properly.

If you are a U.S. Citizen or Permanent Resident and you have a foreign-sounding name, I would suggest putting your status in parentheses under your contact information (ex. (U.S. Citizen) or (Permanent Resident)). This may preclude a recruiter from assuming you will need sponsorship to work in this country. If you are in the lengthy process of applying for Permanent Residence or U.S. Citizenship, I would put your application status in parentheses under your contact information.

An example of the Name and Address section is shown in Figure 7.

Jane Smith	
734-555-1212	185 Arctic Lane
jsmith@umich.edu	Ann Arbor, MI 48105

Figure 7: Name and Address

2 Objective Section

The Objective section is very important because it immediately conveys three pieces of information in one line. The Objective line should show: 1) type of position desired, 2) field of work, and 3) availability date.

The "type of position" is either an internship (3-4 months), a co-op (6-8 months), or a full-time job.

The "field of work" denotes your school Major or a field of study within your Major. The Objective field of work should be broad and at a high level so that you do not exclude any hiring opportunities that might be available to you.

The "availability date" is usually negotiable with the hiring manager. However, for internships and co-ops, it is best to keep the "availability date" close to the end of the term to allow you to complete more work during the assignment. For full-time positions, it is acceptable to push the date out a couple of months if you want to take off some time after graduation. An example of an Objective section for an Internship is shown in Figure 8.

> **OBJECTIVE**
>
> Seeking an internship in Computer Science.   Available: May-Aug, 2013

Figure 8: Objective (Internship)

An example of an Objective section for a Co-op is shown in Figure 9.

> **OBJECTIVE**
>
> Seeking a co-op in Computer Science.   Available: May-Aug, 2013

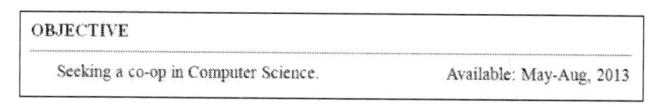

Figure 9: Objective (Co-op)

An example of an Objective section for an Internship which is preferred or a Co-op is shown in Figure 10.

> **OBJECTIVE**
>
> Seeking an internship (prefer) or co-op in Computer Science.   Avail: May, 2013

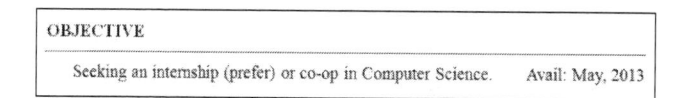

Figure 10: Objective (Internship or Co-op)

An example of an Objective section for a Full-time position is shown in Figure 11.

> **OBJECTIVE**
>
> Seeking a full-time job in Computer Science.   Available: May-Aug, 2013

Figure 11: Objective (Full-time Position)

3a Education Section

For Engineering students, the Education section should be near the top of the resume following the Objective section. Your degrees and schools are listed from most recent to oldest. For example, if you received your BS degree and are currently enrolled in a MS degree program, the university for the MS degree would be listed first followed by the university for the BS degree. The date listed for each degree program is the expected Graduation Date or the actual Graduation Date, if you have finished that degree.

There are many variations to the Education section and all of them depend on your individual circumstances. The following Education examples are shown:

1. BS Degree from one university
2. BS Degree with a transfer from another school
3. BS and MS Degrees from the same university
4. BS and MS Degrees from different universities
5. BS and/or MS Degrees with study abroad
6. Dual Degrees from two affiliated universities
7. Joint Degrees from two affiliated universities

BS DEGREE FROM ONE UNIVERSITY

The simplest Education situation is attending a university for a BS degree. An example of this is shown in Figure 12. As the example shows, it is good to show some relevant coursework and whether you received any honors (ex. Dean's List) for specific terms.

EDUCATION	
University of Michigan, Ann Arbor, Michigan	Apr, 2014
B.S.E., Computer Science, Minor in Economics	
GPA = 3.45/4.00	
Dean's List: 2011, 2012	
Significant Coursework:	
• Database Theory (484) • Network Theory (386)	
• Advanced O-O Programming (371) • Compiler Design (411)	

Figure 12: Education (BS Degree)

BS DEGREE WITH SCHOOL TRANSFER

In parts of the United States, it is common to attend a community college or junior college and then transfer to a four-year university. This is shown in Figure 13.

```
EDUCATION
  University of Michigan, Ann Arbor, Michigan              Apr, 2013
  B.S.E., Electrical Engineering
  GPA = 3.3/4.0
  Significant Coursework:
     • Filtering and Detection (484)      • Circuit Design (332)
     • Image Processing (371)             • Digital Processing (411)

  Washtenaw Community College, Ypsilanti, Michigan      Sep - May, 2011
  Coursework in Electrical Engineering
  GPA=3.9/4.0
```

Figure 13: Education (Community College Transfer)

A student might also transfer from one university to another university to complete the degree. This is shown in Figure 14.

```
EDUCATION
  University of Michigan, Ann Arbor, Michigan              Apr, 2013
  B.S.E., Electrical Engineering
  GPA = 3.7/4.0
  Significant Coursework:
     • Filtering and Detection (484)      • Digital Processing (411)

  Purdue University, West Lafayette, Indiana       Sep, 2010 - Dec, 2011
  B.S, Electrical Engineering with Distinction
  GPA=3.8/4.0
  Dean's List and Semester Hours
  Significant Coursework:
     • Image Processing (371)             • Circuit Design (332)
```

Figure 14: Education (University Transfer)

BS AND MS FROM SAME UNIVERSITY

Students who are attending the same university for both their BS and MS degrees can list the university name and information once for both degrees as shown in Figure 15.

```
EDUCATION
    University of Michigan, Ann Arbor, Michigan
        M.S.E., Electrical Engineering                              Apr, 2014
        GPA = 7.9/9.0 (Scale: 9.0=A+, 8.0=A, 7.0=A-)
        Thesis: "Analyzing Asynchronous Arrays"
        Significant Coursework:
            • Filtering and Detection (484)      • Circuit Design (332)
            • Image Processing (371)             • Digital Process (411)

        B.S.E, Computer Science                                     Apr, 2012
        GPA=3.5/4.0
        Dean's List = 2011, 2012
```

Figure 15: Education (BS/MS from Same University) (Style 1)

Alternatively, the university can be shown separately for each degree, as shown in Figure 16.

```
EDUCATION
    University of Michigan, Ann Arbor, Michigan                     Apr, 2014
    M.S.E., Electrical Engineering
    GPA = 7.9/9.0 (Scale: 9.0=A+, 8.0=A, 7.0=A-)
    Thesis: "Analyzing Asynchronous Arrays"
    Significant Coursework:
        • Filtering and Detection (484)      • Circuit Design (332)
        • Image Processing (371)             • Digital Processing (411)

    University of Michigan, Ann Arbor, Michigan                     Apr, 2012
    B.S.E, Computer Science
    GPA=3.5/4.0
    Dean's List = 2011, 2012
```

Figure 16: Education (BS/MS from Same University) (Style 2)

BS AND MS FROM DIFFERENT UNIVERSITIES

A student getting a BS and MS degree from different universities would need to show each university separately, as shown in Figure 17.

EDUCATION

University of Michigan, Ann Arbor, Michigan — Apr, 2013
M.S.E., Electrical Engineering
GPA = 7.9/9.0 (Scale: 9.0=A+, 8.0=A, 7.0=A-)
Significant Coursework:
- Filtering and Detection (484)
- Image Processing (371)
- Circuit Design (332)
- Digital Processing (411)

Purdue University, West Lafayette, Indiana — Dec, 2010
B.S, Electrical Engineering with Distinction
GPA=3.8/4.0
Dean's List and Semester Hours

Figure 17: Education (BS/MS from Different Universities)

BS AND MS WITH A STUDY ABROAD

At many universities today, students are encouraged to have a study abroad experience. Working or studying in a different country can be a very valuable experience. As a recruiter, I find students who have studied abroad often develop an awareness of diverse groups of people and cultures which is very valuable in the work place.

An example of how to show the study abroad experience for students getting their BS degree is shown in Figure 18.

EDUCATION

University of Michigan, Ann Arbor, Michigan　　　　　　　　　Apr, 2013
B.S.E., Computer Science, Minor in Economics
GPA = 3.45/4.00
Dean's List = 2011, 2012
Significant Coursework:
- Database Theory (484)
- Advanced O-O Programming (371)
- Network Theory (386)
- Compiler Design (411)

Berlin Institute of Technology, Berlin, Germany　　　　Sep, 2012 – Jun, 2012
Study Abroad (Junior Year)
Focus Area: Global Engineering Cultures

Figure 18: Education (BS Degree with Study Abroad)

An example of how to show the study abroad experience for students with both BS and MS degrees is shown in Figure 19.

```
EDUCATION
University of Michigan, Ann Arbor, Michigan                                  Apr, 2012
M.S.E., Electrical Engineering
GPA = 7.9/9.0 (Scale: 9.0=A+, 8.0=A, 7.0=A-)
Significant Coursework:
    • Filtering and Detection (484)      • Circuit Design (332)
    • Image Processing (371)             • Digital Processing (411)

Purdue University, West Lafayette, Indiana                                   Dec, 2010
B.S. Electrical Engineering with Distinction
GPA=3.8/4.0
Dean's List and Semester Hours

King's College, London, England                                    Sep, 2009 – Mar, 2010
Study Abroad (Global Macro Economics)
```

Figure 19: Education (BS/MS Degree with Study Abroad)

DUAL DEGREES FROM TWO AFFILIATED UNIVERSITIES

It is becoming more common for larger universities with established Engineering programs to team up with schools that do not have Engineering programs. For example, the University of Michigan has a dual degree program with Spelman College in Atlanta, Georgia. An example of how to show the dual degree program between two affiliated universities is shown in Figure 20.

EDUCATION

Atlanta University Center Dual Degree Engineering Program

University of Michigan, Ann Arbor, Michigan   Apr, 2014
B.S.E., Aerospace Engineering
GPA=3.45/4.00
Significant Coursework:
- Aerodynamics (414)
- Active Aeroelasticity (372)

Spelman College, Atlanta, Georgia   Jun, 2013
B.S.E., Mathematics
GPA=3.7/4.0
Significant Coursework:
- Graph and Ring Theory (481)

Figure 20: Education (Dual Degrees, Affiliated Universities)

JOINT DEGREES FROM TWO AFFILIATED UNIVERSITIES

It is also becoming more common for a university in the United States to team up with a foreign university to provide a joint degree program. For example, the University of Michigan has a joint degree program with the Shanghai Jiao Tong University in Shanghai, China. An example of how to show this Joint Degree Program is shown in Figure 21.

```
EDUCATION
University of Michigan - Shanghai Jiao University Joint Institute

    University of Michigan, Ann Arbor, Michigan                Apr, 2014
    B.S.E., Computer Science Engineering
    GPA=3.45/4.00
    Significant Coursework:
        • Database Theory (484)
        • Advanced O-O Programming (371)

    Joint Institute, Shanghai Jiao University (UM-SJTU JI), China   Jun, 2012
    B.S.E., Electrical and Computer Science Engineering
    GPA=3.7/4.0
    Significant Coursework:
        • Data Structures (281)
```

Figure 21: Education (Joint Degree between Two Affiliated Universities)

3b Education Special Topics Section

The following specific Education topics are covered:

1. Majors, Minors, University Honors, MS Thesis
2. Showing Junior Standing on the Resume
3. Course Titles and Numbers, Significant Classes
4. When to Show the GPA on the Resume
5. Cumulative or Overall GPA and Major GPA
6. GPA Precision and Scale

MAJORS, MINORS, HONORS, AND MS THESIS

If you have a Major and one or more Minors, these should be listed in the Education section.

If you have received University Honors or have been on the Dean's List, you should list these tributes in the Education section. Majors, Minors, and university honors are shown in Figure 12 on page 33. These are the only types of honors that should go in the Education section. The rest of your awards should go in the Honors and Awards section later in the resume.

If you have written a Master's Thesis, you can list the title in the Education section as shown in Figure 15 on page 35.

SHOWING JUNIOR STANDING

If you have earned Sophomore or Junior Standing when you are only a Freshman or Sophomore, you can state this on your resume. Students attain Sophomore Standing as a Freshman or Junior Standing as a Sophomore when they start college with existing college or AP course credits. As a recruiter, I treat Freshmen and Sophomore Standing Freshmen and Sophomores and Junior Standing Sophomores in basically the same way. Students with Sophomore Standing or Junior Standing generally do not have the same depth as true Sophomores and Juniors.

There are many recruiters who may not understand the terms "Sophomore Standing" or "Junior Standing" and they may incorrectly assume that you have as much experience as a true Sophomore or Junior. This could lead to a student receiving an opportunity normally reserved for Juniors and Seniors. While this might seem like a good thing, you may have to compete with students in the workplace who have more skills than you do. Junior Standing is shown in Figure 22.

EDUCATION

University of Michigan, Ann Arbor, Michigan　　　　　　　Apr, 2015
B.S.E., Computer Science, Minor in Economics (Junior Standing)
GPA = 3.45/4.00
Dean's List: 2012, 2013
Significant Coursework:
- Intro to Databases (281)
- Basic O-O Programming (211)
- Intro to Networks (202)
- Intro to Data Structures (214)

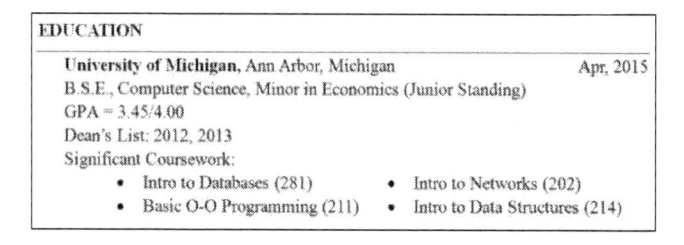

Figure 22: Education (BS Degree with Junior Standing)

COURSE TITLES, NUMBERS, AND SIGNIFICANT CLASSES

Minimally, the courses you list should include the course title. Optionally, you can also include the course number. A course number above 300 usually indicates a more advanced course and that will look good on your resume. The recruiters who come to campus will often recognize both the names and numbers of the courses listed.

It is unnecessary to list every course you have ever taken in your Major. Instead, you should only list the courses that are relevant to the jobs you are seeking. Also, if you take the introductory course followed by the advanced course (ex. Introduction to Data Structures followed by Advanced Data Structures), then you should only list the advanced course. On the other hand, if there is a sequence of courses (ex. Database Management (432), Web Database Design (433), Advanced Topics in Database Technology (533)), then it would be good to list all three courses to indicate that you have depth in this area of your Major.

SHOWING GPA ON YOUR RESUME

Your GPA should always be listed on your resume. You may hear various rules of thumb regarding when the GPA should be shown or not shown on the resume. For example, some advisors tell students that if the GPA is above 3.3/4.0, then it should be shown, and if it is below 3.3/4.0, it should not be shown. These strategies are all nonsense. The recruiter must know your GPA to consider you for a position in his or her company.

When the GPA is not shown on the resume and you are standing in front of the recruiter at the Career Fair, the recruiter will either have to ask you for your GPA or will not consider you for an interview. Even worse, if you are not standing in front of the recruiter to answer this question, then the recruiter will discard your resume outright because the recruiter will not have the time or interest in tracking you down to ask for your GPA. There are many companies that have minimum GPA rules (ex. GPA above 3.0/4.0), but not listing the GPA on your resume is not going to change whether they will accept you for a position.

If you are getting an MS degree, the recruiter will likely be more interested in your GPA for your MS degree than the GPA for your BS degree. However, if you are in the first term of your MS degree, you will not yet have a GPA, so you should put the GPA from your BS degree on your resume.

OVERALL GPA AND MAJOR GPA

It is okay to include both the Cumulative or Overall GPA and the Major GPA when there is a significant difference between the two GPAs. If there is little difference between the overall GPA and the Major GPA, then I would only include the overall GPA. As a recruiter, I am only interested in the cumulative or overall GPA, and most companies will only record the overall GPA in their recruiting database systems.

If you decide to put both the overall and Major GPA on your resume, you need to be prepared to tell the recruiter why there is a difference between the two GPA numbers. If you are only showing your cumulative or overall GPA on your resume, then it is unnecessary to write "Cumulative GPA" or "Overall GPA". You can just write "GPA".

GPA PRECISION AND SCALE

When you show your GPA on your resume, it can have one or two decimal points (ex. 3.4 or 3.45), but I would not show three decimal points (ex. 3.454). Also, it is a good idea to show the GPA scale along with the GPA (ex. 3.45/4.00).

There are some universities that use special GPA scales, especially in their graduate schools. For example, the University of Michigan Graduate Engineering School uses a 9.0 scale where 9.0=A+, 8.0=A, and 7.0=A-. If the scale is unusual like the 9.0 scale, you can either convert the GPA to the more common 4.0 scale, or you can explain the scale as is shown in Figure 17 on page 36.

4	Work Experience
5	Research Experience and
6	Academic Projects Section

The Work Experience, Research Experience and Academic Projects sections follow the Education section. As a recruiter, I value these sections in this order:

1. Work Experience
2. Research Experience
3. Academic Projects

I have seen some students who have gone to school year-round without working for a real company or doing any research projects. As a recruiter, I would say this is not the best way to approach college and generally not an advantage when looking for a position. There are skills you develop when you work in a company, work for a Professor, or work on a research team that are not easily learned through academic coursework. It is very difficult to position a student who has not acquired some practiced, real-world skills, with a hiring manager. A balanced approach involving both work, research and academics is best for most students. There are no hard and fast rules to determine how you combine Work Experience, Research Experience, and Academic Projects. However, these guidelines can help you determine how to utilize these three sections.

WORK EXPERIENCE SPECIFICS

I consider Work Experience to be positions held at real companies. The work can be paid or unpaid. Usually, the work is for an internship, a co-op, or a full-time job. In Engineering, it is rare to have an unpaid work position, but it can happen under certain circumstances. Work Experience can also include paid positions at the university. For example, you could work in the I/T department supporting university computer services.

For each job position under Work Experience, you should show the name of the company, the location, and the dates that you worked there. You should also show your title in that position. Finally, you should provide a few bullets to describe your work at the company. The bulleted lines should be concise and each should fit on one line. They should not extend into the far right column which is reserved for dates. The gridlines in Figure 3 on page 21 show how you can avoid running your bulleted lines into the date column. These gridlines do not show up in the text version of the resume.

An example of how to show Work Experience is shown in Figure 23.

WORK EXPERIENCE

Tolstoy Networks, San Jose, California　　　　　　　　　May – Aug, 2012
Software Intern
- Led a team of 4 engineers to develop a monitor
- Presented performance results to management team
- Designed performance simulator in Java

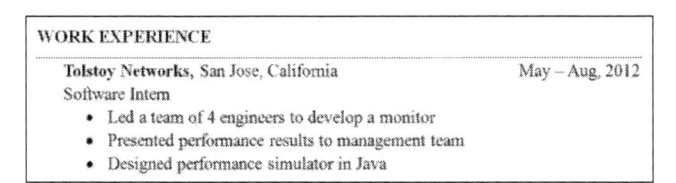

Figure 23: Work Experience Example

As a recruiter, I like to see students with Work Experience on their resumes because this shows me that they have developed some of the real world skills that are needed to work in a company. In any permanent job environment, it is likely that you will work on a team composed of a diverse group of people, with a team leader, and a manager.

The bulleted points for your assignment can show a description of the assignment, the teamwork involved, and the results of the project. If there was a presentation given at the end of the assignment, this is also good to show because it demonstrates your ability to communicate your work.

There are some questions I may ask you about your Work Experience. For example, I may ask if you received an offer to return to the company, or I may ask if you are still working for the company while you are back at school. I use these questions to determine if the company valued your work enough to want you to return or to keep you working during school. In both cases, these are very good signs that you will do well in my company. The last question I ask is, "Did you enjoy your job at the company?" I use this question to determine if you got along with others, demonstrated good teamwork, and were able to sell your ideas.

RESEARCH EXPERIENCE SPECIFICS

Research Experience includes any positions in which you worked with Professors on their research or you worked in research laboratories. A research position can provide you with a deeper understanding of your field of study. Since Professors often have funding and personal relationships with a variety of professionals in industry, the Professor's recommendation of your work can often lead to a position in a company. For international students with Visa restrictions, research positions provide good alternatives to getting jobs in industry.

Research Experience projects should be listed in the same format as Work Experience on the resume. For each project, you should show the name of the research institution, the location, and the dates of your work on that project. It is very important to list the Professor's name and title. If the research project has its own title, you can list it too. If the research is sponsored by a specific company or group of companies, you can list their names if the information is not confidential. The bullets for your research project should show any publications, patents, or talks that were directly related to your work. An example of Research Experience is shown in Figure 24.

RESEARCH EXPERIENCE	
University of Michigan, Ann Arbor, Michigan	Jan – Dec, 2012
Advisor: Prof. Sam Sath, Pelk Collegiate Professor of EECS Research Project: *"Vertical Scans of Elevated XML Indices"* • Created model to compare relational and XML indices • Developed software to simulate elevated XML indices • Performed experiments and classified results	

Figure 24: Research Experience Example

As a recruiter, I am going to ask you about your work on the research project. I will want to know if the Professor would give you a good recommendation. I may ask if your research assignment was extended which I would consider a sign that the Professor appreciated your work. I may also ask if you teamed up with other researchers on the project.

ACADEMIC PROJECT SPECIFICS

An Academic Project is a course assignment. It can be currently underway or already completed. However, it should not be a project that has not started yet. The assignments listed should support your interests and you should be able to talk about each project in great detail. Generally, you want to focus on assignments from your more advanced courses.

The Academic Projects you list should be both interesting and exciting to you. You should primarily list projects that show how you successfully completed a challenge. The projects may have been group assignments showing good teamwork. Each Academic Project should show the university name, location, and date. It should also show the specific title of the course and the project name. You should list a few bullets describing the project, your approach to solving it, and your solution to the project. An example of an Academic Project is shown in Figure 25.

ACADEMIC PROJECTS

University of Michigan, Ann Arbor, Michigan

Database Theory (484): *"Index an XML Database"* — Fall, 2012
- Created relational and XML object mappings
- Developed algorithm to remove sparse cell groupings

Operating Systems (332): *"Multi-threaded Thread Library"* — Fall, 2011
- Implemented a memory manager to ensure concurrency
- Developed latching algorithm to minimize locking

Figure 25: Academic Project Example

As a recruiter, I am going to ask you about any project you list so you should be prepared to talk about it.

GUIDELINES FOR FRESHMEN

As a recruiter, I understand that most Freshmen have not worked much in the engineering field. Sometimes, Freshmen have work experiences from high school, but these jobs are often not related to their engineering degrees. It is also more difficult for Freshmen to be selected for research projects at the university.

For Freshman resumes, it is acceptable to list work experience from High School whether or not related to Engineering, along with one or two Academic Projects as shown in Figure 26.

WORK EXPERIENCE
Skyline Theaters, Chelsea, Michigan   Jun – Aug, 2010
   Usher
- Collected tickets from customers
- Checked for problems in film quality and sound

ACADEMIC PROJECTS
University of Michigan, Ann Arbor, Michigan
Introduction to Data Structures (142): *"Inverted Hash Tables"*   Fall, 2012
- Developed inverted hash table without using Java classes
- Developed the same structure using Java class library

Figure 26: Freshman Work Experience and Academic Project

GUIDELINES FOR SOPHOMORES

Recruiters know that it is difficult for Sophomores to get internships or co-ops in an engineering field after only one complete year at the university. Sophomores have had more required courses than Freshmen so there are more opportunities to list Academic Projects. My recommendation is to list Work Experience from the summer after the Freshman year or from High School whether or not it is in the engineering field. If there is no Work Experience to list, then use one or two Academic Projects in place of the Work Experience. An example of this is shown in Figure 27.

ACADEMIC PROJECTS

University of Michigan, Ann Arbor, Michigan

Introduction to Data Structures (142): *"Inverted Hash Tables"* Fall, 2012
- Developed inverted hash table without using Java classes
- Developed the same structure using Java class library

Introduction to Algorithms (183): *"Using JDBC and SQL"* Fall, 2011
- Developed database program with JDBC and SQL
- Implemented program using relational database system

Figure 27: Sophomore Academic Projects Only

GUIDELINES FOR JUNIORS/SENIORS

By the time you are a Junior or a Senior, it is important to show Work Experience on your resume and it should not be from your high school years. If you have only one internship or co-op and no Research Experience, then it is good to include one or two Academic Projects, too. This is shown in Figure 28.

ACADEMIC PROJECTS
University of Michigan, Ann Arbor, Michigan
Database Theory (484): *"Indexing an XML Database"*   Fall, 2012
- Created relational and XML object mappings
- Developed algorithm for sparse cell groupings

Operating Systems (332): *"Multi-threaded Thread Library"*   Fall, 2011
- Implemented an memory manager to ensure concurrency
- Developed latching algorithm to minimize locking

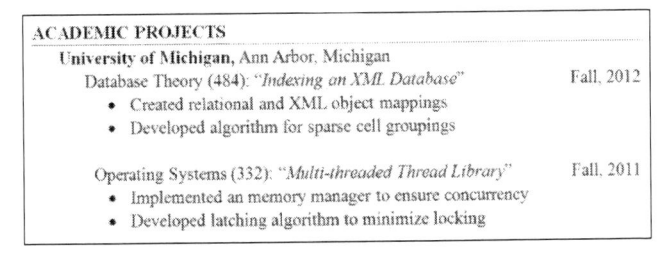

Figure 28: Junior/Senior Work Experience, Academic Projects

In some universities, there is a major project due during the senior year. For example, at the University of Michigan, it is called the "Major Design Project", while at the University of California in Irvine, it is called the "Senior Design Project".

This project is an excellent assignment to list under Academic Projects as it often involves teamwork, creativity, and a great deal of effort to complete. An example of this is shown in Figure 29.

WORK EXPERIENCE

Tolstoy Networks, San Jose, California May – Aug, 2011
Software Intern
- Led a team of 4 engineers to develop a monitor
- Presented performance results to management team
- Simulated performance protocols with Java program

ACADEMIC PROJECTS

University of Michigan, Ann Arbor, Michigan
Major Design Project (481): *"Sparsely Populated XML groups"* Fall, 2012
- Worked with four Seniors to develop XML model protocol
- Developed algorithm to remove sparse cell groupings

Operating Systems (332): *"Multi-threaded Thread Library"* Fall, 2011
- Implemented a memory manager to ensure concurrency
- Developed a latching algorithm to minimize locking

Figure 29: Senior Work Experience and Major Design Project

GUIDELINES FOR GRADUATE STUDENTS

For graduate students seeking Master's degrees, it is important to show Work Experience in your resume. It is possible you will have more than one internship or co-op and you should show all of the jobs you have held in your field of study. If you have Research Experience, it is good to show this too. If there is still room available in your resume, you can show Academic Projects. The academic project should preferably be from your Master's coursework, but it can also be your senior design project. An example of this is shown in Figure 30.

WORK EXPERIENCE

Tolstoy Networks, San Jose, California   May – Aug, 2012
Software Intern
- Led team of four engineers to develop a monitor
- Presented performance results to management team
- Simulated performance protocols with Java program

Dumas Database Systems, Boston, Massachusetts   May – Aug, 2010
Software Development Intern
- Developed algorithm for large table space insertions
- Worked with team to improve command protocols
- Developed software apparatus to improve simulations

RESEARCH EXPERIENCE

University of Michigan, Ann Arbor, Michigan   May – Aug, 2011
Advisor: Prof. Samuel Mast
Project: *"Vertical Scanning Multi-dimensional XML Indices"*
- Created model to compare relational and XML indices
- Developed software to simulate vertical scans
- Performed experiments and classified results

Figure 30: MS Work Experience and Research Experience

GUIDELINES FOR INTERNATIONAL STUDENTS

For international students who are unable to get Work Experience due to their F1 Student Visa status, it is a good idea to apply for a Research position with a Professor. The Research Experience, together with one or two Academic Projects, is a good alternative to not having any Work Experience. This is shown in Figure 31.

RESEARCH EXPERIENCE	
University of Michigan, Ann Arbor, Michigan	May – Aug, 2012
Advisor: Prof. Samuel Mast	
Project: *"Vertical Scans of Elevated XML Indices"*	
• Created a model to compare relational XML indices	
• Developed software to simulate vertical scans	
• Performed experiments and classified results	
ACADEMIC PROJECTS	
University of Michigan, Ann Arbor, Michigan	
Database Theory (484): *"Indexing an XML Database"*	Fall, 2012
• Created relational and XML object mappings	
• Developed algorithm for sparsely covered cell groupings	
Operating Systems (332): *"Multi-threaded Thread Library"*	Fall, 2011
• Implemented a memory manager to ensure concurrency	
• Developed latching algorithm to minimize locking	

Figure 31: Research Experience and Academic Projects

7 Leadership Section

If you have held some leadership positions, it is good to include a Leadership section in your resume. A leader is often viewed by recruiters as self-driven and self-motivated. In some cases, leaders need to deal with conflict resolution and mediation.

Through leadership positions, students can demonstrate maturity and independence, which are considered positive skills by many recruiters. Many hiring managers are concerned when students require a great deal of "hand-holding" during their assignments; managers prefer employees who demonstrate initiative and self-reliance.

Table 1 contains a list of some leadership positions which could be mentioned in a resume.

Table 1 Leadership Positions:

Activity	Leadership Position Examples
Student Group	1. President 2. Vice President 3. Social Organizer 4. Committee Chair 5. Treasurer
Fraternity/Sorority	1. President 2. Treasurer 3. Officer 4. Member of Judicial Board
Volunteering	1. High school tutor 2. Mentor for students 3. Community service project chair
Campus and University	1. Marching band section leader 2. Residential Advisor 3. Graduate student instructor 4. Undergrad student instructor
Professional	1. Military officer 2. President of own company

An example of the Leadership section is shown in Figure 32.

LEADERSHIP	
University of Michigan, Ann Arbor, Michigan	
Introduction to Data Structures (280)	Fall, 2012
Undergraduate Student Instructor (UGSI)	
• Led a discussion section with 23 students	
• Addressed questions on lecture material and assignments	
Local Chapter of National Society of Black Engineers (NSBE)	Fall, 2011
Treasurer	
• Handled dues and local budget for yearly activities	

Figure 32: Leadership Section

8 Skills Section

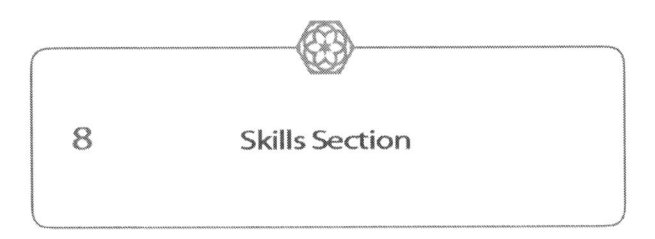

In the Skills section, you show the skills that are important to your Major or field of study in Engineering. It is fine to show skills that you currently have or are in the process of acquiring, but you should not show skills that you will acquire in the future.

It is good to separate skills into recognizable categories. A list of categories and skills is shown in Table 2.

Table 2: Skills Examples

Category	Skill
Computer Languages	- Java - C++ - C - Objective C - .NET - C# - Perl - Matlab - Python - Ruby on Rails
Databases	- DB2 - Oracle - MySQL - Microsoft Sequel Server

Environments	• IMS • Microsoft Access • UNIX • Android • Windows • Linux • Mac OS • iOS • OS X • z/OS
Web Programming	• JavaScript • HTML • CSS
IDE/CAD	• VHDL • Verilog • Eclipse • Xcode • Multi Sim • Quartus
Applications	• Adobe Photoshop • Illustrator • Dreamweaver • Microsoft Office
Spoken Languages	• Spanish • Hindi • Cantonese

An example of the Skills section for a student majoring in Computer Science is shown in Figure 33.

```
SKILLS
    Computer Languages:   Java, C++, C, Objective-C, Perl, XML
    Databases:            Oracle, MySQL
    Environments:         UNIX, Linux
    Web Programming:      JavaScript, HTML, CSS
    Spoken Languages:     Mandarin
```

Figure 33: Skills Section

9 Honors and Awards Section

Ending your resume with the Honors and Awards section will leave the reader on a positive note. This section is often missing from resumes because students are reluctant to acknowledge their own accomplishments. When you list your honors and awards, you are showing the recruiter that you are proud of your achievements.

Some universities recognize when a student has had a good academic term by putting them on the Dean's List or recognizing the student with Semester Honors. I would put these awards into the Education section as shown in Figure 12 on page 33.

I would list all other accomplishments in the Honors and Awards section. Your entries in this section can come from your university or high school years, but you should refrain from including any awards from middle school.

A list of award examples that could be included in the Honors and Awards section is shown in Table 3.

Table 3: Honors and Awards Examples

Honors and Awards Examples
EPICS-AMD, Excellence in Team Performance Award
China Undergraduate Mathematics Content (3rd Place)
University of Iowa EECS Outstanding Service Award
Tolstoy Networks Systems Scholarship Recipient
University of Michigan Engineering Leadership Award
National Merit Finalist
Shin Kong Life Foundation Scholarship Recipient
Singapore Corporation, "2011 New Technology Award"
Valedictorian of Middletown High School
Wisconsin Division I State Golf Champion
Big Ten Men's Volleyball Freshman of the Year
ACM National Programming Contest (2nd Place)
Regional Math Field Day Competition (1st Place)
National High School Chess Tournament (5th Place)
Spelling Bee High School Competition (3rd Place)

A sample Honors and Awards section is shown in Figure 34.

HONORS AND AWARDS	
• China Undergraduate Mathematical Contest (1st Place)	Dec, 2012
• Shin Kong Life Scholarship Foundation Recipient	Apr, 2011
• Singapore Corporation, "2011 New Technology Award"	Jan, 2011
• ACM National Collegiate Programming Contest (4th place)	Dec, 2010

Figure 34: Honors and Awards Section

Ph.D. Resumes

The Ph.D. resume includes most of the sections in the BS and MS resume with the exception of Academic Projects. Here is a list of some additional sections that can be included in a Ph.D. resume (in this order):

1. Dissertation
2. Patents
3. Fellowships
4. Grants
5. Certifications
6. Publications
7. Conference Abstracts
8. Conference Presentations

> **1**   Dissertation Section

The primary focus of the Ph.D. resume is the Dissertation. It should be included in the Education section and it should contain a four to five sentence abstract. It is important to include the full name and title of your Ph.D. Advisor. An example of this is shown in Figure 35.

```
EDUCATION
    University of Michigan, Ann Arbor, Michigan                         Apr, 2014
    Ph.D, Computer Science
    Advisor: Samuel Huggins, Shust Professor of Computer Science
    Dissertation: "Identifying Transformations in XML Indices"

        This dissertation demonstrates that a hierarchical abstraction
        of an XML database system can be simplified by first map-
        ping the relational meta-data. We define the transformation as
        a mapping of meta-columns and demonstrate iteration through
        sequencing over complex structures. We introduce the concept
        of "XML Index Transformation" and demonstrate that each
        atomic property persists in subsequent levels of abstraction.

    University of Michigan, Ann Arbor, Michigan                         Aug, 2010
    M.S.E., Computer Science
    GPA = 7.9/9.0 (Scale: 9.0=A+, 8.0=A, 7.0=A-)
    Advisor: A. Lyon, Basel T. Simons Professor of Computer Science
    Thesis: "Analyzing Asynchronous Arrays in XML Indices"

    University of Michigan, Ann Arbor, Michigan                         Jun, 2008
    B.S.E., Electrical and Computer Science Engineering
```

Figure 35: Ph.D. Dissertation Section

2 Patents Section

It is common to complete a Ph.D. without acquiring any patents. However, if you have received one or more patents or have some patents that are in the application process, these should be shown in the Patent Section, as shown in Figure 36.

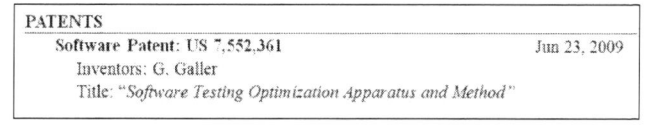

PATENTS	
Software Patent: US 7,552,361	Jun 23, 2009
Inventors: G. Galler	
Title: *"Software Testing Optimization Apparatus and Method"*	

Figure 36: Ph.D. Patents Section

3 Fellowships Section

If you have received one or more fellowships at your university, you can list them in the Fellowships section, as shown here in Figure 37.

FELLOWSHIPS	
2012 Ford Foundation Fellowship Program University of Michigan, Computer Science	2012

Figure 37: Ph.D. Fellowships Section

4 Grants Section

It is good to list any grants that pertain directly to your research on your Dissertation or to research you did at the university, as shown in Figure 38.

GRANTS	
National Science Foundation (NSF), (CCR-977524) University of Michigan funding for workshop on XML Indices	May, 2011
National Science Foundation (NSF), (INT-125524) Funding for software and systems conference in Berlin, Germany	Sep, 2010

Figure 38: Ph.D. Grants Section

5 Certifications Section

It is less common for Ph.D. students to have passed specific certifications during their time at the university. However, if you did complete some certifications, they should be listed in this section as shown in Figure 39.

CERTIFICATIONS	
IBM Certified Solution Developer	Jan, 2008
XML 3.4 Database Administrator	
IBM Certified System Administrator	Jun, 2008
XML 3.4 System Performance Analyst	

Figure 39: Ph.D. Certifications Section

6 Publications Section

There are well-established standards for listing publications in a resume. Although the standards do not require it, for better readability, I suggest separating the information across multiple lines. An example of this is shown in Figure 40.

PUBLICATIONS	
Database Technical Resource (DTR) Authors: J. Smith, B. Smithen, J. Lickey, X. Gan, A. Worthington Title: *"Examining XML from the Source Level"* Issue: 27(11), 1079-1101	Aug, 2012
ACM Multimedia Systems Authors: J. Smith, B. Strangelove, J. Workey, X. Gan, T. Pavela Title: *"Isolating the XML Transformation"* Issue: 10(2), 179-184	May, 2012
Computer Graphics Bulletin (CGB) Authors: J. Smith, B. Randall, S. Wagner, X. Gan, W. Alveystein Title: *"Relating XML Indices with Relational Indices"* Issue: 14(16), 83-101	Dec, 2011

Figure 40: Ph.D. Publications Section

7 Conference Abstracts Section

If you were one of the listed contributors to a Conference Abstract, then this should be listed in this section. An example of this is shown in Figure 41.

CONFERENCE ABSTRACTS	
IEEE Symposium on Database Systems, Washington, DC Authors: J. Smith, B. Smithen, J. Lickey, X. Gan Title: *"Examining XML from the Source Level"*	Aug 19 – 25, 2011
ISMRM 17th Scientific Exhibition, Berlin, Germany Authors: J. Smith, J. Workey, X. Gan, T. Pavela Title: *"Sequencing the XML Hierarchy"*	May 2 – 5, 2011

Figure 41: Ph.D. Conference Abstracts Section

8 Conference Presentations Section

If you were a presenter at a conference, then you should list this information in the Conference Presentations section as shown in Figure 42.

CONFERENCE PRESENTATIONS	
14TH **European Software Conference**, Graz, Austria Title: *"Demonstrating Decay in XML Sequencing"*	Mar 4 – 8, 2011
Information Software Symposium, Los Angeles, California Title: *"Sequencing the XML Hierarchy Through Iteration"*	Nov 21 – 25, 2010

Figure 42: Ph.D. Conference Presentations Section

6

Career Fair

Career fairs are held on many Engineering campuses in both the Fall and Winter terms. The career fair is a convenient way for companies to find students for interviews and for students to look for full-time and summer employment. They are also a great way for students to identify companies that share their career interests. I always advise students to attend all of the career fairs from Freshman year through Graduate school. Talking to recruiters is a learning process and it takes some time to gain confidence in your conversational skills.

Attending the career fair significantly improves the chance of getting an interview with a company and that can lead to getting a job. I am much more likely to give an interview to a student I meet at the career fair. When students comes to talk to me in person at the career fair, it shows more motivation and I appreciate their efforts to come and speak to me.

If you have identified a few companies that you are really interested in working for, then you should try to visit their tables at the career fair. The career fair is also a great time to write down recruiter contact information for future reference and help.

Your success at the career fair is entirely based on your preparation. If you are prepared to answer the recruiter's questions, you will appear confident and will leave a positive impression. This will significantly improve your chance of moving forward with the company. The time you have with each recruiter is very short. If the career fair is crowded, you typically have between 45 and 60 seconds per recruiter contact so you have to be ready with your resume, your questions, and your responses to the recruiter's questions.

The Keys to Making Use of the Career Fair

1. Know the Different Types of Recruiters
2. Good Questions to Ask Recruiters
3. Talking about Your Multiple Majors
4. Know the Jobs for your Major
5. Preparation for International Students
6. What Recruiters Can Ask International Students
7. What International Students Can Ask Recruiters
8. Multiple Recruiters from Same Company
9. What Do You Do When it is Your Turn

1 Know the Different Types of Recruiters

When you understand the different kinds of recruiters that participate in a career fair, you can tailor your pitch accordingly. For example, you would not want to give a highly technical pitch to a Human Resources (HR) recruiter. At the same time, you wouldn't want to give a non-technical pitch to a regular employee who recently graduated from your program.

The term "recruiter" is used for any company representative who is visiting the campus. A "recruiter" can be an HR employee, who recruits full-time. They may have relationships with multiple schools in a region. Their job is to organize events, work with the career centers, work with student groups, and talk to students at career fairs. Some HR employees will also interview students. Usually, HR recruiters are not very technical so you need to impress them in non-technical ways.

A recruiter can also be a full-time manager. In some cases, managers are also "hiring managers" which means they are looking for students to fill jobs in the managers' own departments as well as openings in other areas of the company. Usually, a manager attending a career fair has an affiliation with the university because it is the school the manager attended. Companies like to send recent alumni to universities because the alumni know the program, the school, and many of the professors. Managers can be very technical if they worked in their field of study before going into management. Sometimes managers are primarily good "people" managers with little technical expertise. You can determine the technical proficiency of a manager during your conversation.

A recruiter can also be a regular employee who is not in management and does not have any authority to hire students. They may be recent graduates of the university with first-hand knowledge of both the classes and the professors. The company may rely on these recent graduates to recommend students that would be good hires. Recent graduates can talk easily with students. Their impressions are passed over to the managers attending the career fair. When you meet a recruiter who is a recent graduate, it is a good idea to look for ways to connect with them, by discussing common professors or courses you both took.

2. Good Questions to Ask Recruiters

As students, you should have your own questions in mind to ask recruiters. For example, you can always start with, "What courses are important for me to take for your company?" Companies often do joint research with the university and have special relationships with specific professors. A good question to ask a recruiter is, "Are there any specific professors that you know here that I should do research with? You can also ask, "Are there any specific research topics that are currently important for your company?" When I receive good questions like these from students, I think they are prepared and interested in my company. Your questions may be just as important as the recruiter's own questions in getting an interview.

3 Talking about Your Multiple Majors

As a recruiter, I have seen just about every combination of Major and Minor degrees on resumes. I am never surprised to see students with multiple talents or interests. To have been accepted by your Engineering School, you must have been very talented. While having multiple talents and interests might seem enviable, it can actually restrict the number of places you can work in a company.

When you have multiple Majors and Minors, you need to decide ahead of time which one you want to focus on before you talk to a recruiter. It is not the recruiter's task to find you the perfect job that fits all of your interests. I had a student tell me he was majoring in Computer Science, Music, and Physics, and he wanted to find a job in my company that combined all of these interests. You should not assume the recruiter has the time, interest, or knowledge to make this happen for you.

A better approach is to focus on which of your Majors would match best with the job opportunities available to you. You don't have to abandon your other Majors or Minors. They will broaden you as a thinker and a team player. Sometimes, you can just turn them into hobbies once you start your job. For example, I majored in Computer Science with a minor in English. Today, I am a technical specialist in Database Technology and a recruiter of Computer Science students for my company; and, on the side, I have written a book.

4 Know the Jobs for your Major

Your Major will determine the field of engineering that you will study at the university. You will complete courses on these topics and become very good technically. However, for each field of study, there can be many different types of jobs you could hold in industry. For example, if you are getting a degree in Computer Science, you could become a software developer writing code, a service engineer debugging customer problems, a quality engineer testing new versions of a product, a requirements engineer identifying pain points for the content of the next version of a product, and many other types of positions.

Prior to talking to a company, you should understand what types of positions are available for your degree and which ones you find interesting. You can find this information on the Internet, by talking to your professors, from discussions with alumni of your school, while on your internship or co-op, by reading posted job descriptions, or at the university career center.

5 Preparation for International Students

If you are an international student (on an F1 Student Visa), then the odds of finding a job at the career fair are diminished, especially if you are working on a BS degree. The odds improve if you are working toward a MS degree and are even better if you are in a Ph.D. program.

While international students can take summer internships without any sponsorship using Optional Practical Training (OPT), many companies know that they can only permanently hire the international student if the company is willing to sponsor the student for full-time work. The extra cost, effort and uncertainty of the sponsorship process makes many employers unwilling to hire international students for internships or co-ops. As an international student, your challenge is to find companies that are either not concerned about bringing you back for a full-time job or are willing to sponsor you after you graduate.

International students are encouraged to broaden their social circles beyond other international students and activities to expand the number of hiring opportunities available to them.

6 What Recruiters Ask International Students

The US government has developed the following two questions that recruiters are required to ask to determine Visa status:
1. Are you legally authorized to work in this country?
2. Will you now or in the future require sponsorship for employment?

These are questions that you need to be prepared to answer at the career fair. With your OPT, you are legally authorized to work in this country. However, your OPT is limited in duration and you will eventually require sponsorship to stay in the United States for full-time employment.

7 What International Students Can Ask Recruiters

After recruiters have determined your Visa status with the two questions, they will tell you whether they are interested in following through with you for an internship, co-op, or full-time position. When recruiters say they cannot work with you, there is nothing to be gained by arguing with the recruiter. The recruiter is most likely simply applying the company policy.

There are some good questions you can ask the recruiter even if the company has a restrictive policy. You can ask, "Do you have any opportunities for international students that are not represented here today?" If it is an international company, you can ask, "Do you have any opportunities for me in my home country?" Some companies have programs that put international students in touch with recruiters in their home countries, especially in the emerging countries of India and China.

You can ask a recruiter, "Do you know of any other companies at the career fair that have opportunities for international students?" As a recruiter, I have many opportunities to speak with other recruiters and I may know exactly where you should focus your time.

8 Multiple Recruiters from the Same Company

Some companies, especially large companies, will send multiple recruiters to the career fair. Each recruiter may be from a different division of the company and they could have different hiring needs. Even within the same company, each recruiter may have different rules for whom they can hire.

As students, you shouldn't assume the recruiters are sharing resumes with each other. A recruiter might be rushing off to the airport following the career fair and have no time to share resumes. When you see multiple recruiters for the same company, you can ask if each recruiter is hiring for different positions and whether it is a good idea to speak to more than one of the recruiters at the table. When a recruiter specifically recommends that you speak to another recruiter at the table, then you should follow his or her advice. The first recruiter probably saw something in you that would be of interest to the other recruiter.

9 What Do You Do When It Is Your Turn

Depending on the size of the career fair, students often have to wait in line for one company for a very long time. Unfortunately, this limits the number of recruiters you can speak to during the day. When you do reach the front of the line, you need to use your time with the recruiter to highlight your strengths.

Typically, the recruiter will take about 10-15 seconds to size up your resume. I use this time to form a mental timeline of what you have done during college by looking at the courses you have taken and your summer work experience. I then ask you whether you are interested in an internship, or co-op, or a full-time position. I also ask you about the kind of work you would like to do in my company. The rest of the conversation is specifically about you and it is your opportunity to convince me to take you to the next step in the process.

Through the discussion with the recruiter, it may be determined that you are not a match for the company's needs. For example, you may be a Sophomore and they may be looking for Juniors, Seniors, and Master's students. While it is never a good idea to argue with the recruiter about his or her rules, it is also unnecessary to immediately walk away.

There are plenty of good questions you can ask the recruiter. For example, if you are a Freshman or a Sophomore and the company is looking for older students, you can ask the recruiter, "When I am a Junior or Senior, what will you be looking for on my resume?" You can ask, "Are there any classes you would like to see on my resume when I am a Junior or Senior?" Also, you can ask, "Do you know of any companies that are similar to yours that are looking for Freshmen or Sophomores?"

I think you should always ask the recruiter to comment on your resume to see whether you are on the right track for an eventual position in his or her company. I had one student come back to me three straight years (6 career fairs) before I gave him an interview. By the second year, I started to remember him and I appreciated his persistence. As students, you can use these multiple visits to the same recruiters to learn how to eventually move on to the next step with the company.

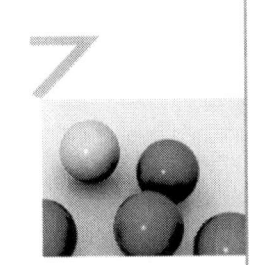

Interviewing

7

Interviews are secured in several ways during the recruiting season. Companies will come to campus for career fairs, information sessions, resume reviews, and student/recruiter mixers. It is a good idea to carry multiple copies of your resume to each of these events. Recruiters will also review resumes online. University career centers will provide access to resumes and student organizations often provide their resume books to company recruiters. You need to make sure your most current resume is on file at your career center and in all available resume books.

Many companies use a process of pre-selection to fill interview slots instead of allowing students to sign up on a first-come basis. It is common for students identified in the pre-selection process to ignore the opportunity. If you keep your eye on the pre-selection dates for each company, and you take some initiative, you can often get an open time slot even if you were not pre-selected by the recruiter.

The Keys to Preparing for Your Interview

1. Research the Company
2. Develop "Tell Me About Yourself"
3. Know how Behavioral Interviews Work
4. Prepare Questions for the Interviewer
5. The Interview Day
6. Know the Next Steps After the Interview

1   Research the Company

It is not difficult to research a small company, but larger companies have many products and different types of work assignments. While some companies use generic job descriptions, you can usually narrow down your research of the company by carefully reading about job openings and by searching on the Internet using keywords in the job descriptions. If you are contacted directly by a recruiter for an interview, you can ask him or her specific questions about the positions the recruiter is trying to fill.

The job description may also show the amount of travel expected in the position. For example, it may show "100% travel" which often means you will live in one city, but work most of the week in another city. It can also mean you will be travelling from one city to the next. In some cases, you may be required to live near one of several large cities. You should be prepared to discuss your willingness and ability to travel.

2 Develop "Tell Me About Yourself"

One of the most common questions a recruiter will ask to start the interview is, "Tell me about yourself". The interviewer is not looking for a response off the top of your head. Your response needs to be well-thought out, prepared and practiced so that it sounds totally natural and believable.

It is not easy to come up with a good 30-second description of your essence. When it is done well, it can provide the interviewer with discussion points for the remainder of the interview, and it can also show the recruiter that you came prepared for the interview. The "off the top of the head" response very often sounds rambling and unimpressive.

CREATE AN OUTLINE FOR "TELL ME ABOUT YOURSELF"

The first step in creating the 30-second response to "Tell me about yourself" is to create an outline. An example is shown in Table 4.

Table 4: Create Outline for "Tell me about yourself"

Outline Topics
1. Your year and Major in the university
2. Your interest in this company
3. One project you liked related to this company
4. Your strengths that benefit this company
5. What you could contribute to the success of the company

FILL OUT THE DETAILS IN THE OUTLINE

The second step is to drill down into your outline by creating a few sub-bullets. An example is shown in Table 5.

Table 5: Drilling into Outline for "Tell me about yourself"

Outline Topics	Specifics (an Example)
1. Your year and Major in school	a. Junior in Computer Science
2. Your interest in this Company	a. Company has a lot of focus on database software b. Company is leader in XML database area
3. One project you liked related to this company	a. In Advanced Database Theory, studied XML databases and XML indices
4. Your strengths that benefit this company	a. Problem solver b. Persistence c. Team player d. Well-organized
5. What you could contribute to success of this company	a. Like to explore new ideas b. Motivated to solve complex problems

TURN OUTLINE INTO A PARAGRAPH

The third step is to turn the detailed outline into a paragraph written in the first person. For example:

> "I am a Junior majoring in Computer Science. I have read about how your company is a leader in database software. I am very interested in your focus on XML databases. I took the Advanced Database Theory course and we did a project on creating indices for XML databases. My strengths are in my problem solving skills and my persistence in working through complex issues. I think your company's focus on XML databases as the next generation of database technology is very exciting. I would like to contribute to your company's success in this area."

READ THE PARAGRAPH OUT LOUD

The fourth step is to practice reading your paragraph several times out loud. It is a good idea to use a timer to ensure your response is close to 30 seconds. My example here was 33 seconds which is good enough. The 30-second response must sound smooth and natural to be believable by the interviewer, so be sure to write the paragraph to reflect how you would normally speak to an interviewer. You can find many examples by searching the Internet with the text "tell me about yourself examples engineering".

3 Know how Behavioral Interviews Work

Behavioral interviews are very common on engineering campuses. They allow both technical and non-technical managers to anticipate how likely you are to succeed in their company. The interviewer measures your answers to a specific type of question. There has been a lot of research on behavioral interviews and whether they can predict whether an applicant will become a successful employee. An accepted set of competencies have been identified as shown in Table 6.

Table 6: Behavioral Interview Competencies

Behavioral Interview Competencies
Communications
Practical Learning
Analysis/Problem Assessment
Judgment/Problem Solving
Teamwork/Collaboration
Initiative
Planning and Organizing/Work Management
Technical/Professional Knowledge
Motivational Fit

With behavioral interviews, past behaviors are used to predict future behaviors. For example, the interviewer may ask, "Tell me about a time when one member of your team did not do his assignment." Your answer to this question could show how you might adjust your work assignments when faced with a difficult team member.

A list of sample questions shown for each competency is shown in Table 7.

Table 7: Behavioral Interview Typical Questions

Competency	Typical Question
Communications	What strategies do you think work to communicate your projects to other people?
Practical Learning	Describe a course project where you needed to learn new information.
Analysis/Problem Assessment	Describe how you break down a project into smaller more manageable pieces.
Judgment/Problem Solving	Describe a problem for which your first ideas for a solution were incorrect and how you determined this.
Teamwork/Collaboration	What do you do when someone on a project is not pulling his or her weight?
Initiative	Describe a situation in which you led a team to solve a problem.
Planning and Organizing	Describe a situation in which you had multiple projects due at the same time and how you managed your time.
Motivation	Have you ever worked on a project that was not interesting?

There are strategies you can use to prepare for a behavioral interview. The most common one is called S*T*A*R:

(**S**)ituation * (**T**)ask * (**A**)ction * (**R**)esult

With S*T*A*R, you describe a Situation you were in or a Task you needed to accomplish, the Action you took to resolve it, and the Result of your work. It is recommended that you think of six to eight recent experiences from your internships or co-ops, academic projects, community service, or team projects. It is a good idea to have half of your experiences be positive and the other half begin negatively with a positive ending. You use these experiences together with the the S*T*A*R strategy to answer the behavioral interview questions.

You can find hundreds of articles and suggestions on the internet if you search for "S*T*A*R behavioral interviews".

4 Prepare Questions for the Interviewer

I am always impressed when a student comes to an interview with a written list of questions. Having questions prepared ahead of time shows the interviewer that you are interested in the company and you thought through the interview. When I interview students, I usually end the interview with, "Do you have any questions for me?" You can search the Internet for questions to ask using the text "best questions to ask an engineering interviewer". A list of good questions to ask is shown in Table 8. A list of questions that you should avoid asking is shown in Table 9.

Table 8: Sample Questions You Can Ask the Interviewer

Questions
1. How would you describe the work at your company?
2. What do new people typically do in their first year?
3. What kind of training does the company provide for new people?
4. What is the typical career path for this position?
5. When do you expect to make your hiring decision?

Table 9: Questions to Avoid Asking the Interviewer

Questions
1. Basic questions about the company that could easily be found on the company website.
2. Personal questions to the interviewer.
3. Questions about salary, vacation, or other benefits.

When you ask your questions, show interest in the answers, listen carefully, and ask appropriate follow-up questions to demonstrate that you value the interviewer's answers. Be aware of the body language of the interviewer so that you can expand or contract your answers appropriately.

5 The Interview Day

The interview day can be very long for the interviewer. Typically, a recruiter has either nine 45-minute interviews or thirteen 30-minute interviews. A 30-minute interview consists of a 20-minute discussion with the applicant followed immediately by ten minutes of private time for the recruiter to complete the interview evaluation. A 45-minute interview might have a 30-minute discussion and a 15-minute evaluation. If you are given the opportunity to select your interview time, it is best to pick a morning slot when the interviewer is fresh. If you have to pick an afternoon slot, then it is best to pick a time just after a break. The worst interview time slot is the first hour following lunch because that is when recruiters are generally tired.

For the interviewer, there are very few breaks and the day moves quickly from one interview to the next. If you are late to the interview, it is unlikely the interviewer will be able to accommodate you because it would throw off his or her entire schedule for the day. If you know you have a conflict with the day or time of the interview, you should contact the interviewer ahead of time to change the interview. It is okay to request a phone interview if you know you are not going to be in town on the day of the interview. It is not okay to miss the interview and then ask for a makeup time on a later date.

It is always a good idea to dress up for an interview. The interviewer may or may not dress up for the interview. In fact, many recruiters wear casual clothes with a company shirt. When you dress nicely for your interview, it shows that you are interested in the job and are taking the interview seriously.

The recruiters for the career fair may be different than the person doing the interviews on campus. An interviewer is often a first-level manager at the company: a hiring manager looking for specific students who meet his or her hiring needs, or managers recruiting for several openings in the company. First-level managers can be technical people or they can be business people. The interviewers can also be trained Human Resources (HR) professionals who are often non-technical people. The type of interview, technical versus behavioral, usually depends on the technical abilities of the interviewer.

The interviewer will identify most of his or her questions from the details of your resume. You should be able to relate at least one interesting story, detail, or example for every academic project, work experience, or course listed on your resume.

6 Know Next Steps After the Interview

At the end of the interview, it is very appropriate to ask the interviewer what are the next steps in the interview process. You can ask "When should I expect to hear from you?" You can also ask, "Can I contact you if I haven't heard back from you?" If the interviewer doesn't provide you with his or her contact details, it is okay to ask for ther interviewer's business card.

Once the interview is over, it is nice to send a "thank you" note to the interviewer providing some details of things you learned or liked about the company during the interview. You can take this opportunity to include additional materials about yourself or to point to your own website.

# 8

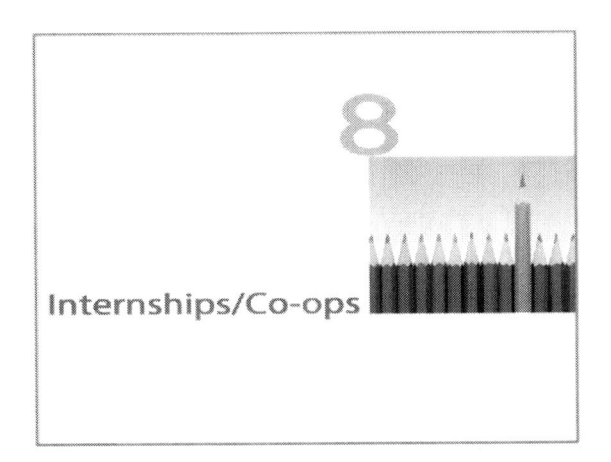

Internships/Co-ops

Internships or Co-ops during college are as important as completing coursework. The skills you need to succeed in college can differ from the skills you need to be successful in a job. When you have an internship or co-op, you have an opportunity to demonstrate that you can work in a professional setting with diverse groups of people, as a team player, within a management structure.

As a recruiter, I have seen some students with excellent grades who decided to go straight through school without any internships or co-ops. This may be an excellent plan if your goal is to get a Ph.D. and pursue a career in academia or in a research facility. However, if your goal is to join a company following graduation, then having work experience during your college years is very important. Most students gain a great deal of knowledge about their employer and their field of study during their internships or co-ops. In addition, one of your primary goals should be to get a positive recommendation from your immediate manager. An offer to return for another internship or co-op or a full-time job is another good primary goal.

The Keys to Successful Internships/Co-ops

1. Knowing Who to Impress
2. Keeping Your Manager Informed
3. Creating Your Status Report
4. Dealing with a Manager Change
5. Continuing Work after an Internship/Co-op
6. Saving Important Contact Information

1 Knowing Who to Impress

It is common for you to have both a manager and a team leader when you have an internship or co-op. The manager leads the entire department. The larger projects may have several team leaders. A team leader is usually an experienced individual who has more knowledge of the project than the other individuals on the team. The team leader provides updates to the manager on the status of the project.

As a student in the group, you will get most of your direction from the team leader. He or she will assign you tasks and point you in the right direction to solve problems. The team leader is often asked by the manager to report on the members of the project and their abilities to complete assignments. The team leader's input is very important and you need to create a very good working relationship with him or her. Ultimately, it is likely to be your immediate manager who will determine the success of your internship or co-op. Managers are responsible for appraising all of the employees in the department. While they will take input from the team leader, the manager will also have his or her own opinions of your work. It is crucial that you develop a good relationship with your manager

2 Keeping Your Manager Informed

Most managers are very busy with project and personnel responsibilities and they don't have much time to spend working with students. Managers spend most of their time in project and management meetings. They need to keep their own higher level managers up to date on the accomplishments, obstacles, and the work of the employees in their departments. Managers value students on internships and co-ops who are self-driven, show some signs of maturity, demonstrate a healthy level of curiosity, are able to ask the team leaders for help with difficult problems, and have the ability to receive and learn from feedback.

While your manager is very busy, it is your responsibility to keep him or her up to date on your work and accomplishments. I suggest that you schedule a 30-minute meeting with your manager either once a week or twice a month. When the meeting is formally scheduled on the calendar, the manager will be more likely to set aside time to speak to you. This meeting is not "off the top of your head". You need to prepare a Status Report that covers all of your assignments and progress in the department. Before your first meeting, I recommend asking a few permanent employees in the department how often they meet with the manager for their status updates and if the manager expects the meetings to follow a specific format.

3 Creating Your Status Report

If the manager does not use a specific format for the Status Report, then I would recommend using the sections in Table 10 to create your own status report. These are the same sections I use in my own status reports.

Table 10: Status Report Sections

Status Report Sections
1. Here is what I am working on now.
2. Here is my current set of problems that I have not yet resolved.
3. Here is what I am doing to resolve these problems.
4. Here is what I am going to focus on next.
5. Am I doing what you are expecting me to do in my assignment?

I recommend that you bring a print-out of your status report to the meeting to allow your manager to take notes during the update. I would also send them the report through email following the meeting so they can file it away for future reference. As you go through your status update, there will be plenty of opportunity for you to receive feedback from your manager. Your ability to listen attentively and then to accept and act on your manager's feedback is very important.

The status update meeting serves two purposes. First, it gives your manager a great record of your work during the internship or co-op. The manager can later use the report to create your final evaluation. Second, it ensures that there are no "surprises" between you and your manager on the manager's expectations for you and your accomplishments during your internship or co-op.

4 Dealing with a Manager Change

While some managers stay in a department for many years, it is more common for managers to make lateral or vertical moves to new departments every few years. Changes in management can occur at any time and your manager may leave during your internship or co-op.

A management change is difficult for everyone in the department. Although it may take some time for the new manager to get up to speed in the department, I recommend that you schedule your status update meetings soon after the new manager arrives. You should never assume that your first manager will tell the new manager about your discussions during your assignment. It is your responsibility to transfer commitments you received from your first manager to the new manager. It is a good idea to summarize your tasks and accomplishments to your new manager during your first status update meeting.

5 Continuing Work after an Internship or Co-op

It is okay to ask your manager if you can continue to work part-time during school after your internship or co-op is over. The manager may like this idea if your project is close to being completed or your expertise is still needed. There is no guarantee that this extra work will result in an offer to return to the company, but it does improve your chances significantly. It is less common to continue working during school but for a new department with a different manager or on a new project… but it can happen.

If you are interested in requesting part-time work after you return to school, it is best to wait until you are close to the end of your assignment. Whether you are on a 3-4 month internship or a 6-8 month co-op, I would recommend waiting for the last month of the assignment. This will give your manager plenty of time to decide and support your request. You can use part of one of your status update meetings to have this discussion with your manager.

6 Saving Important Contact Information

When your internship or co-op is over, you should keep the contact information of your manager, team leader, and key co-workers. It is easy to forget their names and email addresses once the assignment is over. If you are interviewing with the same company, the new recruiter will probably want to contact your previous manager to ask about the quality of your work and whether the manager thinks you should be rehired by the company. You may also want to continue to network with these co-workers after you return to school.

Full-time Jobs

I have several recommendations for things to consider in your full-time job. It may take some time to fully develop your plans and strategies for success since they may involve an understanding of your company environment, processes and rules. Some companies may already have formal policies for some of my recommendations.

The Keys to Successful Full-Time Work

1. Keep Your Manager Informed
2. Think about Your Long-Term Goals
3. Understand How Your Appraisal Works
4. Tell Your Manager You Want a Promotion

1 Keep Your Manager Informed

Your manager needs to know what you are doing so he or she can appraise you at the end of the year. In full-time positions, many managers have weekly or bi-weekly status update meetings with all of the employees in their department. Managers are responsible for the projects under their control so they want to be aware of the tasks being completed in their group.

It is also in your best interests to have regular status update meetings with your manager to keep him or her aware of your work assignments and accomplishments. If your manager doesn't formally invite you to a status update meeting, you should feel free to schedule one with your manager. When you update your manager regularly, you should be able to avoid any surprises during your yearly appraisal.

You can read how to develop your own status report and see the sections I use in my status report in Table 10 on page 116.

2 Think About Your Long-Term Goals

It is good to create a career plan with your long-term goals. This plan contains your ideas of where you want to be in your career in three to five years. The career plan is a living document that should change as you learn more about your interests in your field. You should revisit the plan at least once every year.

Some companies will have formal career plan documents that include a formal discussion with your manager. In these meetings, your manager will learn your long-term career goals and your manager may identify tasks and opportunities in support of your goals. For example, if your career plan shows you are interested in becoming a manager in future years, then you might be given the opportunity to "shadow" an executive.

Whether your company has a formal career plan or not, it is in your best interest to create one so that you continually think about and communicate your career aspirations.

3 Understand How Your Appraisal Works

Your manager will likely explain how your appraisal works. However, if not, this would be a good topic for one of your status update meetings. You want to understand how the company values various activities in your job like teamwork, leadership, problem solving, finishing assignments on schedule, making recommendations, speaking up in meetings, and so on. Once you understand your manager's expectations, you can tailor your status updates to demonstrate your successes.

4   Tell Your Manager You Want a Promotion

There are two key assumptions about promotions that many new-hires make both of which are incorrect. First, they assume that everyone in the department wants to be promoted. Second, they assume that if they work hard and do a good job, the manager will automatically promote them. There are some managers who do watch out for their employees and do ensure everyone is promoted fairly and in a timely fashion. However, ultimately, your career is your own responsibility.

You shouldn't make these two assumptions for yourself. There are some employees who don't want to get promoted because they are happy with the amount of work they have and the level of responsibility in their assignment. If you want to get promoted, you have to let your manager know. When a manager knows you want to be promoted, the manager can look for opportunities for you to demonstrate that you can work at the next promotion level, and in turn, this helps the manager build the case for your promotion. There are budgetary concerns and your manager may have to sell your promotion to the rest of the management team and to their immediate managers. Also, there may be a limited number of promotions allowed per year and managers may have to compete for these promotions for the members of their departments.

Your status update meetings with your manager are good times to discuss your desire to be promoted. You can add a section to your status report that says, "Do I have enough responsibilities in my job to justify a promotion to the next level?" If you ask this question in every status update meeting, your manager will know you want to get promoted and will ensure you are positioned to receive a promotion. You still may not get the promotion, but you will have put yourself in the best possible position with your manager.

10

Conclusion

The recruiting process begins during the Freshman year and lasts through graduation. The keys to success lay within each student's abilities to distinguish himself or herself during the process.

A well-organized and concise resume is essential for every step in the process and it must be updated every semester. It is a student's opening statement to a recruiter.

Preparation and practice are the keys to success at the career fair. Understanding the recruiter's questions and knowing how to respond can lead to interviews for intern-ships, co-ops, and full-time jobs.

To distinguish yourself in an interview also involves preparation, practice, and a thorough understanding of the interview techniques used on many engineering campuses.

Internships, co-ops and research assignments provide training – not just in a student's field of study – but also in learning how to deal with diverse groups of people.

An engineering recruiter looks for students with these acquired skills when they interview students for full-time positions. The students who distinguish themselves are most likely to attain the jobs they desire.